# French Alphabet
# Coloring Book

## Nina Barbaresi

Dover Publications, Inc., New York

*French Alphabet Coloring Book* is a new work, first published by Dover
Publications, Inc., in 1992.

*International Standard Book Number: 0-486-27247-8*

Manufactured in the United States of America
Dover Publications, Inc., 31 East 2nd Street, Mineola, N.Y. 11501

# Preface

THIS BOOK IS DESIGNED to help children learn the twenty-six letters of the French alphabet and 146 French words while they enjoy coloring the illustrations. Each page is devoted to one letter of the alphabet and contains various French words beginning with that letter. At the bottom of each page is an alphabetical list of all the words appearing on that page. This list provides the English equivalents for the French words along with their definite articles (English "the"). In French, there are two gender-indicating definite articles in the singular: *le* (for masculine nouns) and *la* (for feminine nouns). To indicate the plural, the article for both genders is *les*. When a French noun begins with a vowel, the definite articles *le* and *la* are contracted to *l'* (e.g., *l'abeille*, the bee). This is also the case for some words beginning with "h" (e.g., *l'hirondelle*, the swallow). When the contracted form of the definite article is used, the gender of the noun cannot be determined from it. To help children learn the gender of such words, the abbreviations M (for masculine) and F (for feminine) have been given along with the words.

avion

abeille

accordéon

**A**

arbre

araignée

arc-en-ciel

l'abeille (F., the bee); l'accordéon (M., the accordion); l'araignée (F., the spider); l'arbre (M., the tree); l'arc-en-ciel (M., the rainbow); l'avion (M., the airplane)

bateau

bicyclette

ballon

bouteille

balançoire

baleine

la balançoire (the seesaw); la baleine (the whale); le ballon (the balloon); le bateau (the boat); la bicyclette (the bicycle); la bouteille (the bottle)

cheval

cloche

C

chaise

chat

chien

chapeau

la chaise (the chair); le chapeau (the hat); le chat (the cat); le
cheval (the horse); le chien (the dog); la cloche (the bell)

dragon

doigts

drapeau

dents

dindon

les dents (F., the teeth); le dindon (the turkey); les doigts (M., the fingers); le dragon (the dragon); le drapeau (the flag)

enfants

école

écureuil

étoile

église

éléphant

l'école (F., the school); l'écureuil (M., the squirrel); l'église (F., the church); l'éléphant (M., the elephant); les enfants (the children); l'étoile (F., the star)

feuille

fenêtre

fromage

fraises

fourchette

fleurs

la fenêtre (the window); la feuille (the leaf); les fleurs (F., the flowers); la fourchette (the fork); les fraises (F., the strawberries); le fromage (the cheese)

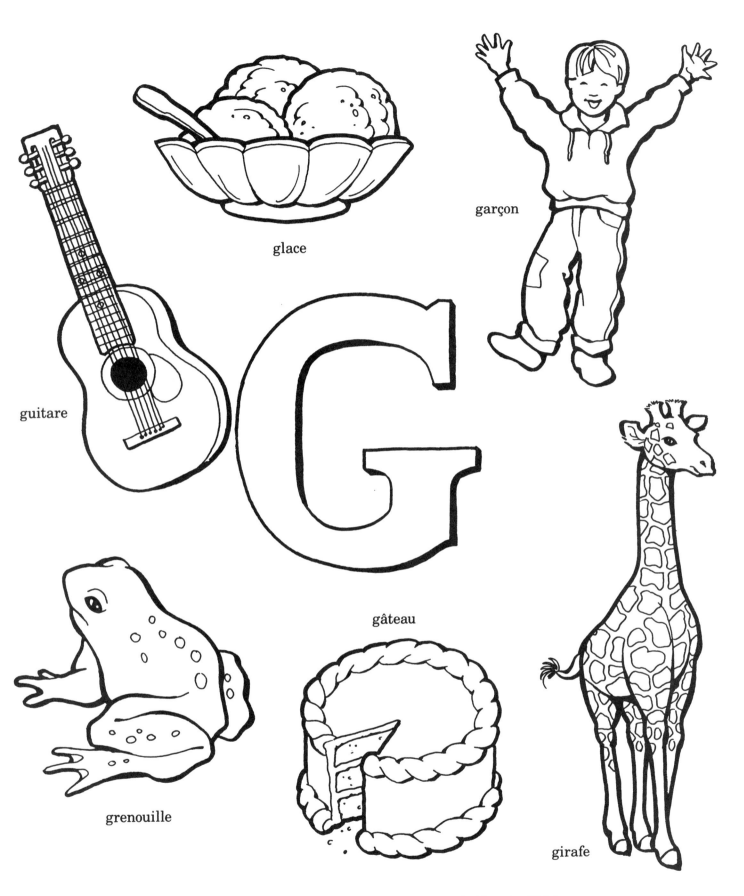

glace

garçon

guitare

G

gâteau

grenouille

girafe

le garçon (the boy); le gâteau (the cake); la girafe (the giraffe); la glace (the ice cream); la grenouille (the frog); la guitare (the guitar)

11

hibou

horloge

hache

houx

homme

hirondelle

la hache (the ax); le hibou (the owl); l'hirondelle (F., the swallow); l'homme (M., the man); l'horloge (F., the clock); le houx (the holly)

iguane

île

insecte

I

igname

igloo

ibex

l'ibex (M., the ibex); l'igloo (M., the igloo); l'igname (F., the yam);
l'iguane (M., the iguana); l'île (F., the island); l'insecte (M., the
insect)

journal

jardin

jupe

jambe

jumeaux

jouets

la jambe (the leg); le jardin (the garden); les jouets (M., the toys);
le journal (the newspaper); les jumeaux (M., the twin brothers);
la jupe (the skirt)

kiwi

kayac

kimono

K

kiosque

kangourou

koala

le kangourou (the kangaroo); le kayac (the kayak); le kimono
(the kimono); le kiosque (the kiosk); le kiwi (the kiwi); le koala
(the koala)

lapin

lettre

livre

lunettes

lune

lion

le lapin (the rabbit); la lettre (the letter); le lion (the lion); le livre (the book); la lune (the moon); les lunettes (F., the spectacles)

mouche

montagne

montre

**M**

main

maison

médecin

la main (the hand); la maison (the house); le médecin (the doctor); la montagne (the mountain); la montre (the watch); la mouche (the fly)

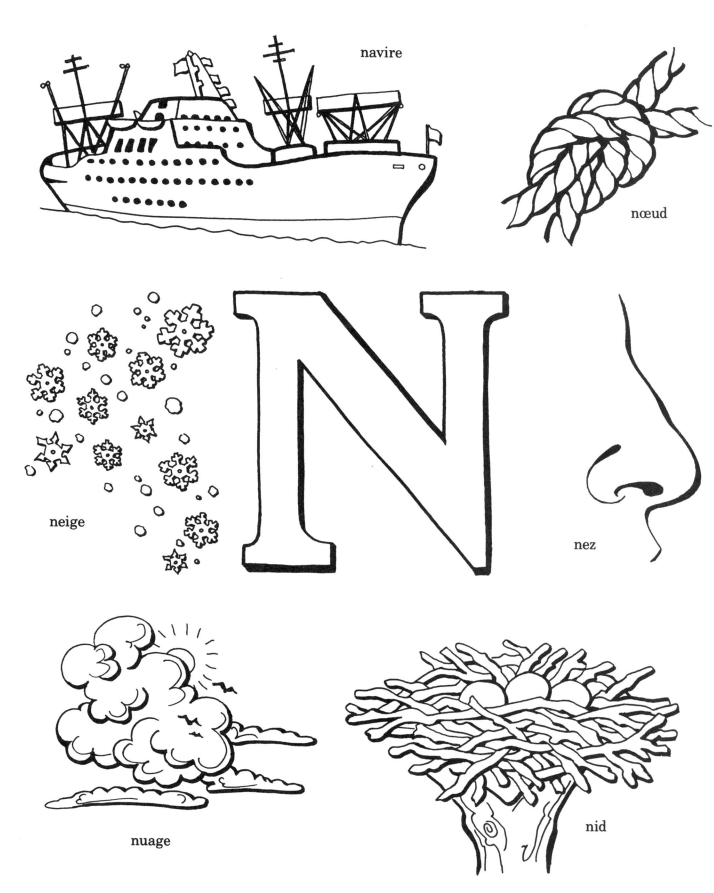

navire

nœud

neige

N

nez

nuage

nid

le navire (the ship); la neige (the snow); le nez (the nose); le nid
(the nest); le nœud (the knot); le nuage (the cloud)

oreiller

oreille

oignon

os

œufs

oiseau

les œufs (M., the eggs); l'oignon (M., the onion); l'oiseau (M., the bird); l'oreille (F., the ear); l'oreiller (M., the pillow); l'os (M., the bone)

19

papillon

pont

pomme

poisson

poupée

parapluie

le papillon (the butterfly); le parapluie (the umbrella); le poisson (the fish); la pomme (the apple); le pont (the bridge); la poupée (the doll)

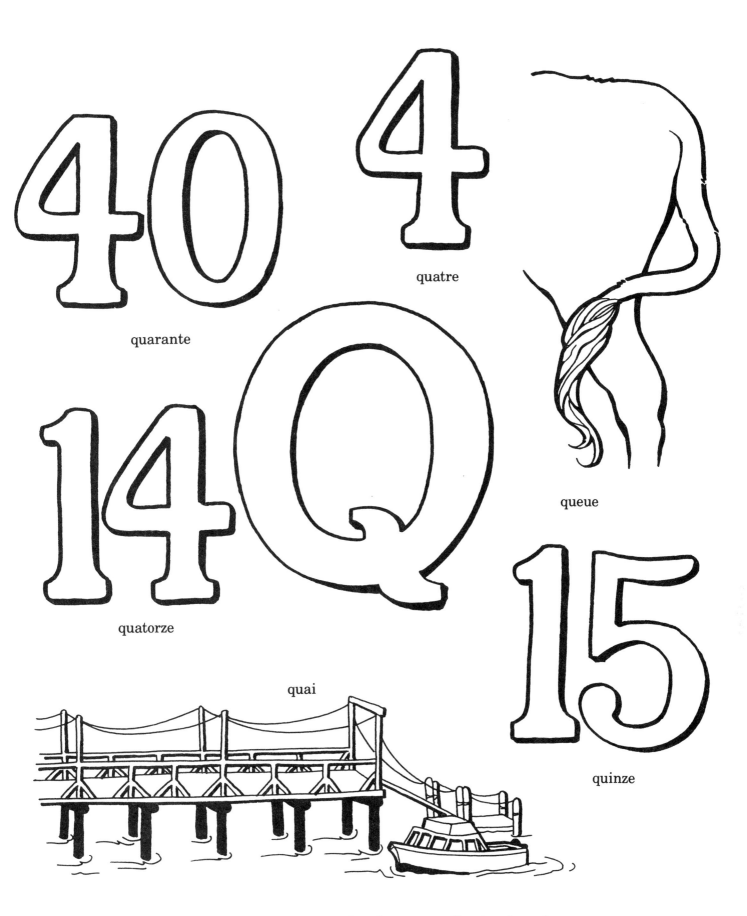

**40** quarante

**4** quatre

queue

**14** quatorze

Q

quai

**15** quinze

le quai (the pier); quarante (forty); quatorze (fourteen); quatre
(four); la queue (the tail); quinze (fifteen)

rose

reine

roi

renne

robe

renard

la reine (the queen); le renard (the fox); le renne (the reindeer);
la robe (the dress); le roi (the king); la rose (the rose)

savon

souris

soleil

seau

S

singe

soldat

le savon (the soap); le seau (the pail); le singe (the monkey); le
soldat (the soldier); le soleil (the sun); la souris (the mouse)

tasse

tigre

tête

T

trompette

train

table

la table (the table); la tasse (the cup); la tête (the head); le tigre
(the tiger); le train (the train); la trompette (the trumpet)

urne

urubu

usine

l'urne (F., the urn); l'urubu (M., the urubu, black vulture);
l'usine (F., the factory)

visage

volcan

violon

verre

ver

vache

la vache (the cow); le ver (the worm); le verre (the drinking glass); le violon (the violin); le visage (the face); le volcan (the volcano)

wagon

wharf

water-polo

western

wapiti

le wagon (the railway car); le wapiti (the wapiti, American elk); le water-polo (water polo); le western (the western film); le wharf (the wharf)

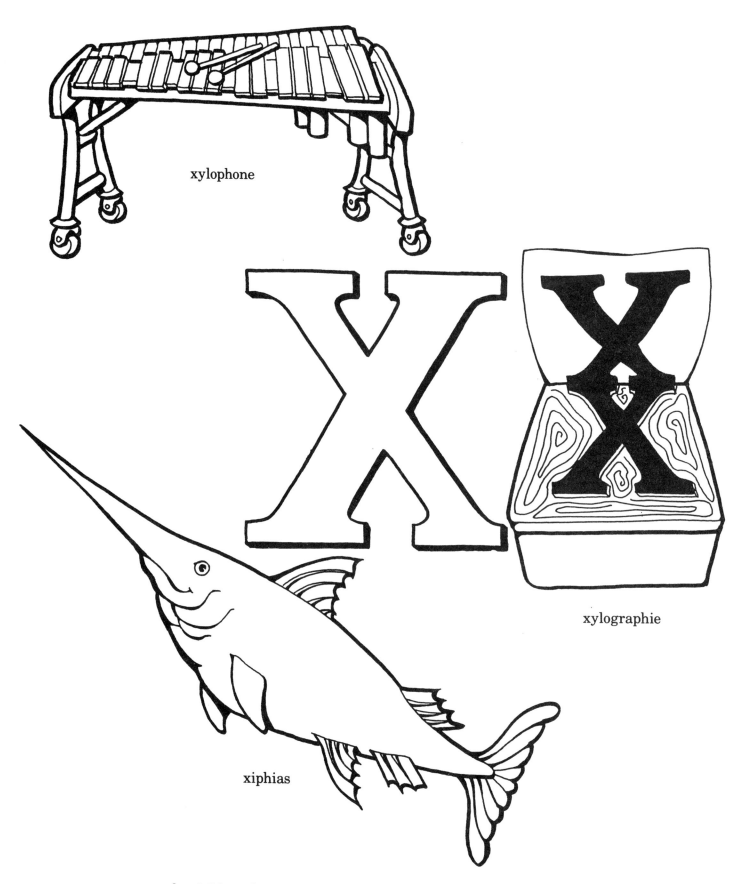

xylophone

xylographie

xiphias

le xiphias (the xiphias, swordfish); la xylographie (the wood-cut); le xylophone (the xylophone)

yourte

yacht

# Y

yucca

yak

yeux

le yacht (the yacht); le yak (the yak); les yeux (M., the eyes); la
yourte (the yurt, Mongolian tent); le yucca (the yucca)

zébu

zinnia

zeste

zèbre

zigzag

le zèbre (the zebra); le zébu (the zebu); le zeste (the zest, lemon peel); le zigzag (the zigzag); le zinnia (the zinnia)